LOVE, HOPE AND MAGIC

Also by Ashish Bagrecha

Dear Stranger, I Know How You Feel

Dear Stranger, You Deserve to be Loved

LOVE, HOPE AND MAGIC

ASHISH BAGRECHA

POEMS

HarperCollins *Publishers* India

First published in India by HarperCollins *Publishers* 2022
HarperCollins *Publishers* India, Cyber City, Building 10-A, Gurugram,
Haryana-122002, India
www.harpercollins.co.in

8 10 9 7

P-ISBN: 978-93-5629-342-7
E-ISBN: 978-93-5629-345-8

Typeset in 10/11.5 EB Garamond
by SÜRYA, New Delhi

Printed and bound at
Nutech Print Services - India

*

HarperCollins *Publishers*, Macken House, 39/40 Mayor Street Upper, Dublin 1, D01
C9W8, Ireland

Dedicated to:

The love, hope and magic of my life,

Savi

'how did you survive all this time?'
'i inhaled pain and exhaled poetry.'

CONTENTS

Love comes

i love with the energy
of the entire universe
inside me
and i'm just searching
for someone who
could take it all in.

- the search

we must remember
that we are mere travelers of life
on our journey to home,
that nothing will matter in the end,
for everything is chaos
except love.

- the truth

love as hard as you can
for we're all made of stardust
and we'll soon turn into stories
no one will remember.

- the reason

the moment i saw your eyes
i realised why people want a forever.

all your darkest secrets, all your deepest scars,
can i have them?
all your strongest lies, all your weakest truths,
can i know them?
all your biggest fears, all your smallest tears,
can i feel them?

do not say me a no,
please don't say a no.
what if, i am your last chance.
what if, i am your last hope.
what if, i am your last love.
what if, i am your last breath.

i want to set you free from your demons.
i want to fill your void with our moments.
i want to find the broken pieces of your soul.
i want to make you once again whole.

- *the proposal*

everything you are
is everything i need.

- you're enough

she asked me
"what's your biggest fear?"

i whispered in her ear
"to be unloved."

"why do you love me?
what makes me different?"

"it's so easy to love you
and that's what makes you different."

"don't love me, i'm an impossible thing.
i may never love you back."
she said.

"like magic, anything is possible."
i smiled.

love is what brings our two dark souls
together.
love is the light between us.

- what is love?

don't teach me
how to make things disappear
or how to turn anything into gold.
just teach me the magic
that will make you mine.

let me be just enough,
neither too much nor too little,
as you're for me.

- little love notes

i'll take you to an open sky
and love you so wildly,
that it would make the stars
fall into the ocean.

ASHISH BAGRECHA

you didn't just touch my heart
you labelled it as yours.

- *you owned me*

wrap me in your arms
kiss me like never before
undress me if you want to
love me till you need to
let our souls collide
let the stars in us become alive.

your existence is enough for me
to wake up in the morning.

- *little love notes*

love me so much
that when
my time comes
death is scared
to tear us apart.

love is growing old with someone
who doesn't let you feel old.

- little love notes

i will dig a grave
in your soul
through my words
and bury my heart
inside it.
your soul can
never escape mine.

ASHISH BAGRECHA

you're poetry
and i am made of you.

- story of my life

i get surprised
when you ask me about love?
i've learnt about love
from the book in your eyes
i've found love
in the sound of your heart
i've written about love
through the words of your soul.

ASHISH BAGRECHA

my depression is afraid of you,
my love.

- *little love notes*

sometimes i look at the sky
and i feel i don't belong here
maybe i'm from another place
another time another universe
so i question why was i sent here
what's the purpose?
but then i find you besides me
and everything makes sense
everything feels right.

"why do you write about us?"

"long after
our stories end,
i want us
to be touched, remembered and loved
in these tiny little pages
i write for you."

ASHISH BAGRECHA

i'm pretty sure
ours is the kind of love
poets write about and
people dream about.

you and i are the biggest fools
made out of love
and made because of love.

it's so beautiful to be with you
i can't believe any of it.
you wrapped in my arms
me listening to your stories
us having a forever.
i know it's true and real
i know it's happening right now
but why do i feel
i'm living just another dream?
why do i fear
someday i'll wake up without you?

i love you
with every fibre of my soul.

- little love notes

Love leaves

i asked her why she is not okay
and she said
no one is okay in this world.
the truth is
we all are different levels
of not okay.

- the beginning of the end

let this distance make you realise,
some people aren't heart-warming
they're a heart-warning.

- a slow realisation

i am your home,
you'll always
come back to me,
always.

- *a hope*

inside my head
lives a dream of us
i've every night,
you whispering my name
i wishing your touch
us wanting each other.

ASHISH BAGRECHA

the skies cry for the sun
the seas die for the moon
the stars chase the planets
and i crave for you.

it's a full moon night
and i'm craving
for your touch
because
it's the only thing
i know
that can give rest
to the chaos i carry
inside my heart.

i made my home
in your flesh and bone.

- where do i go now?

you made me homesick,
for the home i never had.

maybe i can never make you whole
but i can break my heart into pieces
so that every single part of me
loves every single part of you.

sometimes you want
no love no hope
no magic no reason
just the need to feel alive
and for me that's you.

i know we both are damaged
but if you really love me
i want you to take care of yourself,
i cannot hold two broken hearts
inside me.

- i don't understand what you mean

maybe i'll never understand you
but i'll always stand by you.

- i promise

life will never be
as beautiful as poetry
and love will never
be as perfect as we dream,
even though i might not
be able to fix you
and you might not
be able to complete me,
we still need each other
to keep ourselves warm
in this cold dark world.

- don't go

i laugh at people who say
love is blind
i want to tell them
blind are those who never loved.

you tell me
to forget it and move on,
i don't understand
how can i unfeel love
once i have felt it?

you were the book, i always wanted to read.

you'd always teach me something new
make me do something crazier.
you'd not just make me laugh or cry
you'd make me feel alive.
and i loved holding you so close to me
anywhere, everywhere.
you gave me the warmth and feel
of a true friend and a mad lover.

but most importantly,
you'd always keep going and keep me going.
you were the book that never ended.

you were exactly the book,
i wanted to read forever
the book i never wanted to lose.

but now i'm losing you my dearest,
and i can never read anyone after you.

ASHISH BAGRECHA

every time
i decide to leave you,
the entire universe
tells me to love you,
we're trapped in
a beautiful conspiracy.

even if you rip my soul apart
and break every piece of my heart
even if you take my trust
and shatter it to dust
i will still not forget
how to love you.

i may not be able to stop you
when you decide to leave me
but can i ask you to leave behind
a little smile, a little hug
a little kiss and a little love?
i will seize them in my heart
and use them as stars
in the lonely nights to come.

ASHISH BAGRECHA

sometimes you are in love
with moments and not people.
there's a difference but sadly
we fail to understand it.

what if
it was never love
but simply
an illusion of love?
what if we loved
because we had to
and not because
we were meant to?

poetry can never beautify
the way you loved me
and left me
wanting for more.

ASHISH BAGRECHA

i can't find anyone like you
not even close to you
i look for you in everyone
but i fail every single time.
yet i don't feel lonely or sad
i feel happy and proud
the departure doesn't pain
because i loved the best one.

ASHISH BAGRECHA

maybe everything happens for a reason
maybe that's a lie i tell to myself
to forget you.

ASHISH BAGRECHA

maybe we will never meet
but we can still walk together
like parallel lines
to infinity and beyond.

most love stories
turn into either a victory or a tragedy
but some of them simply happen
to keep love alive in us.
they are the most important ones.

- maybe this was that

LOVE, HOPE AND MAGIC

sometimes i like to read the stars
and wonder what's their story?

for whom do they burn inside
and shine bright on the outside?
why do they guide people
when they themselves are lost in darkness?
why do they fall and perish
just to fulfill someone's wish?
when they know the world won't care
if one of them went missing
why do they still appear every night?

that's when i'm reminded
it's what we all do,
not just the stars.

why? for whom? it's a simple story.
for love.

ASHISH BAGRECHA

if you love me
i'll send light
not gifts,
if you hurt me
i'll bleed poems
not blood.

one in a billion times
a dying star explodes
and creates a beautiful nebula.
a place where new stars
begin to form.
and so now i know
why you left me.
so that my heart could die
and give birth to the nebulae of poems
for new lovers to form.

"love comes, love leaves
but why does it pain?"

"pain is the price we all pay for love.
sometimes for not loving enough
and sometimes for loving too much."

Love pains

i'm not scared of pain
i'm scared of not feeling pain.

you were the magic
my heart could never learn.

ASHISH BAGRECHA

"why do you still hold onto love
when you know it's killing you?"

"because i wonder what else can save me
if not love."

they think
intense love gives intense suffering
but i say
intense suffering needs intense love.

ASHISH BAGRECHA

did you know
our cells have memory?
did you know
my heart still remembers you?
after all these years
after all those tears.

- you haunt me

your heart must have split
into a thousand pieces
before you decided to split with me.
for you needed my time
more than you needed my love.

i switch between different apps
i watch countless posts and stories
i scroll, i read, i reply.
and yet between all of it
you are still there on my mind
like the only memory that matters
and no matter how hard i try
i can never delete you.

ASHISH BAGRECHA

i've waited too long,
i want you back
with interest.

i want my fingertips
to stop telling people about you
but they won't listen to me
i want them to rest
but they keep moving
hoping to prove my love
i tell them you're gone
that no letters or poems can bring you back
but they won't give up
every part of my body is numb except them,
i guess they loved you more than i ever did.

is it a blessing or a curse?
i write more when it pains more.

you took away my entire universe
and left me with broken pieces
and unfinished stories,
you knew exactly
what would keep me alive
after you.

stop wasting your time
switching between apps
for a notification
that will not come.
move on.

- note to self

you kept telling me
to find my magic
i kept shouting
"it's you, it's you."
i guess in the end
we both were fools.

ASHISH BAGRECHA

the universe put
the brightest stars in my eyes
and yet i always fell in love
blindly.

- such an irony

even if it would destroy me
a hundred times
i would still crawl back to love.
for i know nothing else
that i can do better
with all my heart and soul in it.

ASHISH BAGRECHA

to put it gently
we call it a heartbreak
in reality
we feel destroyed.

if you hear my voice
calling your name
in the middle of the night
it's because
you have a piece of my heart
buried under your pillow.

ASHISH BAGRECHA

yes i'm broken
but i'm not for sale.

the tragedy of my life
is not the lack of love
it's the fact that
i love too much.
so much love to give
so less people to take.

pain is a reminder
that love is needed.

- note to self

we all want a love
without heartache
without pain or failure
but tell me something
will such a love
be worth remembering?

ASHISH BAGRECHA

95

you broke something
that was already broken
and what happens
when a broken gets more broken?
it turns into pieces
you can never fix.

love is nothing
but a test of time
if it survives, it's true
if not, it's all a lie.

- the realisation

the way you break my heart
and run away,
it's quite an art
i'd like to learn.

every poetry
is a storm raging
in my soul
after you left.

you are never born a poet
neither you can learn to be
you are simply broken so much
that you become one.

i was the rose
whose petals you tore apart
now left with nothing but thorns
waiting to pierce your heart.

- the agony

i'm the one with a bleeding heart
and you're the one showing-off scars.

why did you
conquer my heart
as if it was a kingdom
you wanted to be proud of?
why did you leave after that
chasing another one?

- you're a cruel ruler

every night i stare at the stars
waiting for some magic to happen
hoping they would open up
and absorb me inside them.

i'm not just another human
i'm a storm and
there is a hurricane inside me
raging like a beast,
i won't be gentle or warm
i'll collide with your world
and kill you with love
you never knew existed.

- *the rage*

you don't know
the angst of a broken heart
and the fire it carries within.
it can burn everything it comes across
or give light to everyone who needs.

i'm the moon
that carries fire
within itself,
don't be fooled
by my calmness
i can either decide
to heal you with love
or burn you with rage.

ASHISH BAGRECHA

trapped in my own chaos
i put on a happy face,
giving everything i have
faking everything i can,
waiting for the breaking point
when all of me will turn into ashes
and fly away with the wind
to a place faraway near the ocean
and i finally rest in peace.

some people don't want love
they just want to forget
that they are damaged
and broken.
they keep running and running
until they crash somewhere
they feel okay.
simply to realise
that they are at
the doorsteps of
love again.

- we can never run away from love

i'm a lost star
drifting far away
from my galaxy
struggling to choose,
to either find my way back
or explore the new galaxies.

- the introspection

everyone wants you
to move on
like nothing happened.
but trust me
the pain you feel
the tears you have
the love you lost,
everything is real
don't let anyone else
tell you otherwise.
you deserve the time
to grieve.

- note to self

you ain't healing
because you're afraid
to let the pain go
as it's your only connection
to the one you loved.

- note to self

"you say time heals everything.
but it didn't heal me."

"i know why time didn't heal you."

"why?"

"because you didn't let it."

hidden inside
this world of poetry
there lives an old soul
confined to a new body
trying to remember
what love felt like.

"why are your poems so short?"
"so i can escape the pain of recalling too much."

i know it's weird for a poet
to think like that
but what if love is the reason
we might all die.

- *who am i kidding?*

"she is gone.
why do you still write for her?"

"maybe one day
when i'm gone too
someone would read these poems
and they might believe
in love again.
that's why."

in times like these
when no one really cares
and humanity seems dying
when it feels like
the world is coming to an end
i write about love
not because love can save us
but because i want to save love.

we're all digging our own graves
conspiring our own extinction
with our cold hearts
and indifferent minds.
mark my words,
the world will come to an end
not because of any apocalypse
but lack of compassion and love.
and that's how
we'll all be doomed.

even though it may seem like
but i'm not writing about a broken heart,
i'm writing about a broken world
and the need to fix it.

i am not scared now
the pain has ended,
i am an ocean of memories
i have nothing to hide,
my words have defeated silence
i have nothing to lose,
i am chaos in its most beautiful form
i am the light of a darkened soul.

- the awakening

if pain is a villain,
hope is the hero.
and even though
it may look like
the villain is winning
it never does.
sooner or later
the hero always arrives
the hero always wins.

ASHISH BAGRECHA

Hope arrives

hope is not just a word
it's what will get us through,
hope is not an inspiration
it's what we owe to ourselves.

ASHISH BAGRECHA

life will be hard sometimes
and all you will need to survive
is hope.
because hope is the magic
we all know.

"you don't understand me. you never will."
"maybe i don't. but i'm trying to."

"listen, i don't need you or your pep talks.
nothing you say can inspire me."
"i'm not here to inspire you."

"then?"
"i'm here to fix you."

you maybe broken
but broken is still something,
and what you build out of it
will always turn out to be 'beautiful'.

"i feel empty."

"no, you are not empty. you are filled with pain."

"what do i do? how do i escape it?"

"don't escape pain. embrace it.
and it will dissolve in your soul."

time will blur the memories
and your heart will heal
from everything
you're trying to forget
right now.

you weren't born with a heartbreak,
you won't die with one,
then why live with it?
this world has so much to offer,
you deserve better.

accept, allow.
embrace, evolve.

you handed me
all your broken pieces
but darling,
how do i fix you
when you don't believe in
love, hope and magic?

you've a dark place in your heart
where all your dreams have died
memories are chained
love is buried
and desires are murdered.
a haunted place
even you don't want to visit it yourself.
but believe me
i'm going to make that place my home
and rebuild it
with love, hope and magic.

ASHISH BAGRECHA

your heart is not a bone
which can be broken
and never be fixed again,
it's made of muscles
that may get damaged
but also knows how to heal.

ASHISH BAGRECHA

the truth is
you are at war with yourself
that's why
you find yourself at war with others.

you don't need anyone to shine
you are a sun not a moon.

you don't want peace
you want the chaos and storm
to bring you pain and destroy you.
you don't want to be found or loved
you want to stay lost and be left alone
but i won't let you.
every time you'll walk into darkness
i'll stand right next to you
and dare you
to destroy both of us.

i promised to fix you
i didn't promise
it won't pain.

- i'm sorry

you think
no one can fix you
but you don't know
some prayers are powerful
and some souls know magic.

ASHISH BAGRECHA

if life is temporary,
how can anyone be permanent?
let them go.

ASHISH BAGRECHA

maybe you'll find
peace and beauty in dark
but that doesn't mean
it's worth staying there.
eventually
darkness eats up everything,
eventually
light destroys dark.

they tell me
that no light can enter
or come out of
the blackhole
inside you
but they don't know
the magic of poetry.

"how do i move on?
how do i become happy?"

"dedicate yourself to a purpose
and not a person."

forced smiles
silent screams
lost souls
broken dreams
we hide
what we all feel
its time
we begin to heal.

i know the stars died in you
and that's how you became
the home of darkness.
but i want you to go
into the unknown
and find a new home.
please remember
you're an explorer
of love, hope and magic.

ASHISH BAGRECHA

maybe it's not about
finding yourself,
maybe it's just about
loving yourself.

maybe one day
these poems i write
will make sense to you
and you will believe
in love, hope and magic
exactly the way i believe.
until then
i'll stay here
and help you fix
your broken heart.

i want to be the diary
that holds your secrets
all your confessions
all your darkness
until you're ready
to let them go.

listen to me
happiness is a daily choice,
and not an impossible dream.

that storm in your heart
let it thunder
let it strike
let it rain
let it flood
let it destroy
let it destruct
and in the aftermath
you will find a sunshine
you will find a new life
the storm will cease
and you will find peace.

death will come to you
the very moment when you're of no use
when you've nothing more to give
when no one needs you.
you being alive is the reminder
that somewhere someone out there
is searching for you
that someone still needs you
that you've so much more to give.

the moon reminds me of you
how beautifully you both try
to fight the darkness.

the universe has already written
all the stories
you're going to read, tell and live.
it has already decided
all the people
you're going to meet, love and lose.
all we got to do is
trust the universe and its flow
because it already knows
all the places
you're going to
find happiness, dreams and hope.

just as light must pass through water drops
to form a rainbow
you too must pass through pain
to see the beautiful colors of life.

ASHISH BAGRECHA

no matter how much we deny
there is a little love in all of us
waiting to explode.
the moment our heart stumbles upon
another heart
who deserve us,
we will erupt like a volcano.

we're all scared
to let love in
but love will always
find a way
to touch us
like the rain.

they say
pain changes people
they forget
so does love.

i got broken
and shut my heart,
the pain couldn't find an exit.
years later i realised
i should have left my heart
wide open.

- *the mistake*

you already know
i'm broken beyond repairs
and still you hold me
as tight as you can
without letting me go
simply waiting and wanting
for me to undo the damage
i caused to myself.
damn it,
it's working.

i wonder why would a river like you
love a storm like me.

we're just two people
trapped in love
trying to fix each other
but failing remarkably.
we're just two people
yet holding on to hope.

but darling
why are you so scared?
don't forget
you're a kid of the universe
and it's looking after you.

ASHISH BAGRECHA

what if we are fallen stars
who've forgotten their origin,
and are looking at the sky
trying to remember
what home felt like.

ASHISH BAGRECHA

i always feared love
and then you came.

i wish i could be for you
what you have been for me
a ray of hope
a rain of happiness
a cup of coffee
and a book of love.

you might not believe this
but even without me
you are everything.
don't let anyone
not even me
make you feel otherwise.

ASHISH BAGRECHA

the entire universe is mine
and yet i'm lost
in search of something
to call my home.
how foolish of me.

you put my demons to rest
when i'm tired of fighting them.

promise me
you'll stay alive
so that one day
when i'm in your city
we can go for a coffee
talk about the stars
and share our stories
of love and hope.

promise me
you won't give up
so that the universe
gives us a future
we deserve.

ASHISH BAGRECHA

wherever i went
i never wanted to be seen,
until you happened to me.

ASHISH BAGRECHA

to those who say
this is a generation
of confused minds
lonely hearts
and broken people,
i ask
which one was not?
so don't worry about us,
we too will find our ways
to live, love and heal.

ASHISH BAGRECHA

you lit a fire
to burn my world,
little did you know
the moonlight protects me.

- note to my past

we all have a price
attached to our hearts
some can afford us
some cannot
and some will bargain.
but never ever
lower your price
for those
who don't deserve you
for those
who will own your heart
only to show off
for those who will throw it
when you grow old
and find another brand new heart.
give yourself to only those
who really want you
and will handle you with care
as if they can't live without you.

- *please remember this*

ASHISH BAGRECHA

173

in a universe so vast
we are a drop in an endless ocean
our lives so miniscule
and our breaths so fragile
that nothing we do
would ever make a difference.
none of us will ever reach the end
and no one will be left
to remember our stories.
so why does our lives matter?
why does anything we do matter?

because we love
and the universe runs on love.

if love hurt you
then only love can heal you.
there is no other way.
that's the magic of love.

ASHISH BAGRECHA

humans give hope,
universe gifts magic.

Magic happens

"what if i never find love?"
"don't worry. then, love will find you."

"how?"
"in its own mysterious and magical ways."

"why?"
"because souls like you deserve to be loved."

in the deep black sky
even though a million miles apart
the sun still finds a way
to bring light to the moon,
and you expect me
to leave you in this darkness.

"why are you so scared of coming closer to me?"

"there is a whole universe inside you and i'm just a
little star. what if i lose myself in you?"

how long would you hide in the dark
under the shadows of the moonlight
waiting for the sun to rise.
you need to become the sun
you need to try, you need to rise,
or risk your entire life
living in that darkness forever.

if you're given darkness,
you'll also be gifted with stars.

ASHISH BAGRECHA

you are made of stardust
every inch of your body
was once a part of the galaxy.
when you hate yourself
you hate the universe.

ASHISH BAGRECHA

maybe the reason
why you are feeling restless is
because the universe is trying
to tell you something
and the stars are trying
to talk to you.

- *listen to them*

the moon doesn't leave me
following me wherever i go
guiding me through the dark
as if i am its child
and it is looking after me.

the world has disappointed you
the universe will not.
trust me on that.

ASHISH BAGRECHA

you ask me about myself
you want to know more
but i don't know
how to tell you
that the sky is my life
some stars are my friends
the moon is my love
and the night,
it's my home.

ASHISH BAGRECHA

if all you want is only darkness
then i can rip out all the stars in the sky
but i'm sorry
my heart cannot stop glowing for you.
you can have a starless sky
and a moonless night
but i'm sorry
my soul will always send you light.

ASHISH BAGRECHA

the reason why so many of us get hurt by love
is because our love is an illusion
and after a while illusions always break.
true love is supposed to feel like magic.

ASHISH BAGRECHA

love like magic
has to be
mastered.

- it takes time.

only if we had the eyes
to look through each other
we'd understand
that inside our fractured hearts
we all carry
an exceptional magic
to heal each other.

if the sun doesn't reach you
and you've given up
on the stars and moon,
i'll break myself
into a million pieces
and sprinkle them
across the sky,
to send you light
and save you
from your depth of darkness.

ASHISH BAGRECHA

i wonder how you can feel
my pain, suffering and love
exactly the way i feel it.
maybe that's the magic
we're all born with.

maybe the universe didn't send you
to connect the dots or find answers
to unsolved mysteries of life
maybe you're here
to share the fire you brought within you
with the souls lost in darkness.

ASHISH BAGRECHA

you'll feel weak
you'll fall
you'll get hurt
but i know
you'll never give up,
you're a warrior
with magic in your veins.
you'll always fight.

LOVE, HOPE AND MAGIC

the world can cause me
all the pain it wants
it can take away
every single person i want
it can break
every bone in my body
it can create
every chaos in my mind
but it can't destroy my love
it can't steal my hope,
it can't kill my magic.

ASHISH BAGRECHA

i don't think
i'll ever find the magic
that can show you,
how you saved my life
with your mere existence.

- thank you

sometimes you will fall
so bad like there's no stopping.
a free-fall with no control
into the dark abyss
from where there's no coming back.
but just when you're
about to be sucked into it,
if you'd close your eyes
and think of love
trust me
love will pull you through
in the strangest way
you'd ever imagine,
it'll surprise you
with its magic.

ASHISH BAGRECHA

you may call me
a hopeless romantic
but i refuse to believe
there is no magic
between us.
how in the world otherwise
did i end up with you?

so what i found you
after so many lifetimes
how could i forget
to bring you the light?

- the promise we made

all my life
i've been running after the roads
that may lead me to finding magic
that would fix me.
but only after i met you
i realised
magic runs inside me.

you possess me like
the moon possesses the sky.

sometimes love is
as simple as
watching the moon
with you
and sometimes
it's as difficult as
counting all the stars.

- i love doing both

if the universe could
grant me one wish
all i would want
is for my magic
to reach people
long after i'm gone.
you know how
the light of a star
travels the universe
long after it dies.

ASHISH BAGRECHA

i have stars inked all over my body
in the form of scars
and every time you touch me
they emit light.

ASHISH BAGRECHA

even though we feel
that we live our lives alone
but amidst every heartbreak
every failure every loss
every drop of tear
and every time we gave up
someone was always there
watching upon us.
only if we looked up
from our self-centered lives
we'd realise that
the stars have always been there
living our lives with us
and never leaving us.
we'd realise that
they have been shining
and smiling all this time.
because they already knew
what we didn't.
how one day we would discover
the magic within us.
how one day we would look at them
and smile right back.

ASHISH BAGRECHA

i may've been
struggling all my life
with pain, heart-break
and darkness,
but i've never forgotten
that i'm made of
love, hope and magic.
that i'm the home
of light.

ASHISH BAGRECHA

Magic stays

the magic of our love
is not just in
what we are today
it's in
what we will become.

- a story, a poetry, a forever

when i talk to you
it feels like
i'm talking to the universe,
and i guess
that's why
all my dreams come true.

if the universe decides to
fulfill all my wishes and
complete all my dreams
i would end up
with nothing
but you.

you're the only universe i trust,
the only magic i believe,
the only reason i exist.

"what is your heart made of?"
"stars."

i'll surround you like
the stars surround the moon,
you can never escape me.

now i know
what happens to the stars
when the sun comes out,
they don't disappear
they hide in you.

i love you
because
you have stars in your soul.

you hung the moon,
scattered the stars
and brought sunlight for me.
still you question,
why do i call you my universe?

in every universe,
you're my everything.

you taught me that
i can find stars in life
and universe in people.

ASHISH BAGRECHA

when i look into your eyes
you make me believe in myself
but more importantly
you make me believe in people.
you see it's so important for me
to see you.

ASHISH BAGRECHA

i've carved my name
on your soul,
so if you ever go missing
the universe can return you
to me.

ASHISH BAGRECHA

in another time
in another world
in another universe,
i'd love you
exactly the way
i love you here,
we'd always be home
no matter where
our souls wander.

an endless universe
with endless possibilities
but i promise you this
we will never be strangers again,
i'll always find you.

when i look back
i realize
it was not us
but the universe
who was fighting
for us and
for our forever.

the world will never know
what we went through
to be with each other,
but believe me
the stars are proud of us.

ASHISH BAGRECHA

LOVE, HOPE AND MAGIC

love comes, leaves and pains,
but magic happens and stays,
and all we need is
a little hope in between.

ASHISH BAGRECHA

no one knows
where our spirits go
after they leave us
no one knows
where our homes are,
but i think
maybe when all this ends
we simply become magic
that gets remembered
as stories.

do you know
the biggest magic of the universe?
sooner or later
everyone finds love
that stays.

DEAR READERS

And here we come to the end of another road. Thank you for taking the time to read through my thoughts and feeelings.

I hope you inhale poetry and exhale pain.
I hope you inhale love and exhale magic.

To my readers who have patiently waited for this book, you have no idea how much I'm thankful to you. You are the reason I can continue doing what I love.

Thank you for sharing your lives with me, writing me encouraging messages and critical feedbacks, recommending my books to others and interacting with me on social media.

If you loved this book and have a minute to spare, I would really appreciate a short review on the page or site where you bought the book.

This is my first self-published book and your help in spreading the word is greatly appreciated.

You're all amazing!

With profound gratitude,
Ashish Bagrecha

ABOUT THE AUTHOR

Ashish Bagrecha is a best-selling author and one of the most loved Instagram poets in India.

His books, *Dear Stranger, I Know How You* Feel and *Love, Hope and Magic* have sold lakhs of copies. He is a strong mental and emotional health advocate and voices his experiences and observations through poems and reels which have found a connection with millions of youngsters online.

Ashish is also a popular audio creator and you can listen to his podcasts and shows on Audible and Spotify.

A strong believer in the universe and its magic, Ashish holds a master's degree in marketing and runs an app development agency. He currently resides in Surat and is married to best-selling author Savi Sharma. Together, they dream to heal and inspire millions of souls through their poems and stories.

You can visit him on Instagram @ashish.bagrecha or log on to www.ashishbagrecha.com

If you are someone who is struggling with depression, anxiety, negativity, heartbreak or loss, please read *Dear Stranger, I Know How You Feel*. There are thirty letters and poems for thirty days to help you begin your journey to hope and healing.

The book is available at Amazon, Flipkart and bookstores near you.